The Journey to Happiness

"The light in the dark abyss"

Umar Ashraf

Umar Ashraf

To those who struggle,
but still keep fighting,

To the survivors.

Umar Ashraf

CONTENT

Umar Ashraf

Dedicated to ending depression, anguish, sorrow and anxiety from the depths of your soul. Replacing it with happiness, prosperity, and success.

INTRODUCTION

This masterpiece filled with enthusiasm and motivation is your first and biggest step to overcoming the most daunting spiritual demons known to man. A large part of society walks around the streets with darkness roaming within their souls. When anyone is born, they are born with the right to success, and happiness. With such darkness in their souls, happiness and success seems to be light years away. Some even think that the darkness has consumed them to a point of no return. I, on the other hand believe that happiness and success is just around the corner. This battle is a great war people underestimate greatly. It's not a war you can win by yourself, but you can definetly win this war. That is the purpose of my book, this book acts as a wormhole that will get you to that happiness and success you thought was millions of light years away. The key is to never lose **hope.** Use this book as a guide, as a map to get that happiness and success you deserve ever so greatly. Are you ready to snatch back what was wrongfully taken from you? Are you prepared for the happiness that awaits you? This will be one bumpy ride, but it'll be a ride you wont ever forget.

"Sometimes we go through pain to realise what happiness really is"

CHAPTER 1

HOPE

His heart slowed,

His eyes soaked from the continuous tears,

He threw it all away,

Or so he believed…

He picked himself up from a bay of tears,

Looked himself in the mirror,

And decided to face his fears.

He knew it wasn't time to accept defeat,

He knew he was getting nearer with each step,

He knew… he knew happiness was near.

- Hope in the most desperate times.

- Hidden Hope -

At times, we beg on our knees for mercy, thinking there is no end to pain while we drown in misery. Our faces don't bare a single smile... but what if I told you tomorrow will be better than today, and that the day after tomorrow will be even better than tomorrow. Your first step to happiness is finding the urge to do what you will. Finding hope in the places you never sought.

Have you ever seen a homeless man smile, and wonder, why is he smiling? How is a person who has literally nothing, smiling? He found his lost, hidden hope. If he can do it, I sure as hell have faith that you can too. Hope can be found in the most ridiculous places. You just need to open your eyes, be more aware of your surroundings, and be observant. The more people you see happy, question yourself. If they are happy, then why can't I be happy? Sure, everyone has their own issues. But no issue is too big to jeopardize your happiness. Everything comes to end, your issues come to end, but we don't have to let your happiness come to end. Trust me that smile you're hiding can blind any person within a 5 mile radius. So get out there! Roam around and be free! Find your

Sometimes I wonder, what am I doing?

Does this emptiness last forever?

What if I just turn the lever?

Find the happiness I thought I'd never get?

I can't feel it, can you?

Other people have turned the lever,

Maybe it's time for me too?

This life is contagious,

We ain't falling any further,

This thrill is filled with wonder.

I forgot what the "rough times were"

Is this depression's cure?

- The shimmering lever of happiness.

- Never Again -

Never again will I let the demons speak on my behalf, never again will I keep my mouth shut when someone tells me to be quiet, and never again will I succumb to the calls of sadness. Remember you are never truly alone, people will be your friend! Never again will I keep myself closed to the people around me. Be kind and gentle with them and if they are the same with you, they are the people who will pick you up every time you fall, and every time we fall, we only fall to rise higher than ever. What doesn't kill you, makes you stronger. There is always light at the end of the tunnel. Will I ever lose hope? No…never again.

Make each day your masterpiece. Give your best every single day. Never again will I stay in bed, letting the world revolve around me. I am part of this world, and I will make sure my footprint is visible to every creature, animal, and human. There is always light at the end of the tunnel. Will I ever lose hope? No…never again.

Everything I work for,

Walks out the door,

Death feels like it's the only option,

Oh, I fall apart,

Right down to my core.

People say I will never succeed,

I fall apart to rise,

I can be sad, or I can fight,

Each tragedy makes me even more wise,

In the dark, I am the light,

The tears keep flowing,

But I keep going,

People say I will never succeed,

But watch me proceed to succeed.

- Rise above the blaze of words

- Better Soon -

Heartbreaks, tragedy, and failures. Things that break us down to our core with a pickaxe. Life doesn't make sense, why are the rich, sad? And the poor, happy? Is money the problem? My brain crashes like a computer with a corrupted hard disk. Oh, I fall apart, down to my core, if only I was informed. I didn't know it'd hurt this bad. Life keeps going, today's pain will be tomorrow's pain, but days will come where the clouds dissipate into the air, and a downpour of hope will shower upon the saddened dwellers. One day I will be happy, and maybe it just takes time but I ain't gonna succumb to the demons anymore, I've been through enough pain.

Today I'm running in the open fields, and tomorrow… who knows, I could be six feet deep, be in a wheelchair, or be reduced to dust, I don't know what's going to come tomorrow. Enough faking this forced smile, enough. A wise man said to me, "everyone laughs with you, but ain't no one gonna cry with you." This has been the roughest journey for me, through the potholes and dusty roads, I'm still here, so if god's kept me here through all this, why give up now? I have hope that everything will be better, because if I'm still here, He most definitely has a plan for me. Indeed with time will come happiness. Patient I remain. Strong and steady is what I will

I ain't who I was before

I feel as if I'm stuck in tar,

They wrote a list of dirty words,

I guess it really shows who we really are,

We think words really defy who we are,

Aiming below the bar,

Recognised as an outsider from afar.

Some people's ego fills the distance from ground to the stars.

Sometimes I feel stuck in an emotionless boomerang,

Some people bite you in the back till the base of their fangs,

Happiness is a commodity,

A commodity… I can't afford.

- Hopelessness in a hopeless world

- Paranoid Phases -

I wake up every day, knowing each day is a lifetime. A lifetime of no relief. Tell me why I can't get no relief? Inside of my head a barrage of noises scream throughout my skull. My lungs fill and my rib cage creaks. My voice becomes shallow. My thoughts are hollow. Heavy breathing is what follows. My eyes bleed tears. Blame it on me, it's not my fault I couldn't breathe, I tried to stop it but it just happened. No matter what you believe, I'm telling you it caught me on my knees, it's not my fault I couldn't breathe. Oh, so anxious is my soul, so confused I am. I got too much on my mind right now. I need the world to come to a halt. Or else I believe my heart will be the one at fault.

What you just read was a man screaming for mercy from the grasp of anxiety. Anxiety exists, depression exists, and mental disorders EXIST. We take hits, until were torn to bits. We give up because we think it's too hard. We go through thick and thin for a yearly birthday card. We will always go through thick and thin, small and large, narrow and wide. Only… to rise through the ashes each time. We always do, everyday one little achievement is a victory, getting out of bed is a victory. We rise through the ashes every day, we just await the day the building never burns again. And there will be a day. I promise you that. Have hope because we ain't never goin' back. Because the mountains are ours to conquer. Because the world is ours to rule. Because there will be a time we will smile as a whole. There will be a time…there will be a time.

CHAPTER 2

Faith

Umar Ashraf

Sadness consumed her,

She was stuck deep within a vortex,

Her self-confidence had the same width of a can made of tin,

People said she deserved to rot in the bin,

The words consumed her,

The words repeated in her mind,

Trash, Useless, Worthless,

She believed it wouldn't get better,

She was wrong.

In fact she forgot how she was the only one of her kind,

Little did she know she had the soul of an angel,

She was the one a man would die for,

She was a queen,

She was only a teen,

But she was already in the mind of an adult,

She was perfect.

- The Forgotten Queen

- Belief -

Sometimes we believe the pain will never stop. We believe were a mess that can't be cleaned with a mop. As of this moment I am 40,000 feet up in the air flying over Greenland. Even now I can tell you that no matter what anyone says or what has happened in your life, you are a soldier! You are what you believe you are. This statement has more truth than the "you are what you eat" statement. Once you engrave the thought in your mind that you are a fighter, no word or issue will affect you, some of you may think, "He doesn't know us? How are we even fighters?" Well you are fighting each day for your happiness, each day when you get out of bed you are fighting those demeaning demons that spit negativity in your face. Each day you face problems and hatred etc. but here you are today, alive, breathing. You are a fighter, everyone around you is fighting their own battle. In fact you are why I'm writing this today, you need to be told your fighting has been acknowledged, I'm writing this today so you can actually smile without having to force it. No one deserves pain, and I know how it feels to have nothing, you probably feel the same way sometimes. If I got through this battle, so can you. I believe in you, but do you believe in yourself?

The breeze whistled around his ears,

A lake, formed at his feet from his tears,

He faced his fears,

He was a soldier with no peers,

When he was alone he knew it was going to be okay,

He knew his pain might not dissipate today, tomorrow, or this year.

But he knew this is the place for his permanent stay,

At times he couldn't bare the pain,

He believed everything would be okay with each drop of rain,

Slowly, he cleaned all the stains on his tainted soul,

Because happiness was his ultimate goal.

- The faith of a lone wolf

- The Flight of Faith -

It's okay to fall, it's okay to feel as if you failed, but it is never okay to lose faith in yourself. In order to be happy, you need to have faith in yourself, the ride of believing in yourself and happiness is similar, it's like a flight with turbulence. The ride can have its ups and downs, but it always gets to its destination. On this journey you will learn things you never knew before. You will most importantly learn that you are loved, you are needed, you are amazing, you are someone with the brightest soul, you are beautiful, and this is an adventure you will never forget. One day you won't even realise and suddenly your sadness will be replaced by happiness. I promise you that you will find happiness.

Hate,

Don't matter to me,

But faith… faith,

Is everything to me,

- The power of faith

- Blind Faith -

Sometimes we just leap into things and we don't even think about it. The only thing you should have blind faith in is yourself, you gotta be that legend, you gotta be that stone in history, and nowadays we think that we'll just go with the flow, but for me if I die, ima die as a legend. I'm gonna leave my footstep in this world so I'm never forgotten. I have faith in myself, we all should, at the end of the day if were still here we must be strong enough and special enough to be here. We need to say no to laying around with our feet up. It's about time we show the world who we are. It's time we show those people who say we are useless what we are capable of. But first engrave a strong faith in yourself, because only you and God will have pure faith in you. If you don't have that faith, then you won't get nowhere. But it doesn't have to be that way. Life is a difficult, but we will never go down without a fight. It's a survival instinct.

In the night,

We fight,

But in the day,

We pray,

Do we lose?

We do,

But do we give up?

No,

We don't ever stop.

- The diary of a warrior

- Secure Faith -

Control, control your anger, anytime, all the time. We tend to get angry when we fall, thinking we're done. We lay at the base of the cone. Thinking we're nothing but flesh and bone.

But… we're much more.

We are all soldiers, fighting our own wars,

We are all builders, building our own legacies',

We are all aspirers, aiming for the stars,

We are all students, learning every day,

We are all legends, and we are all gonna die as legends.

Never go down without a fight or a smile on your face. A smile that can blind the 7.8 billion people on this magnificent planet.

CHAPTER 3

Overcoming Heartbreak

I can't get over you,

You left your mark on me,

Remember the times you said "I love you too"?

But maybe it wasn't meant to be,

You were there,

Now you ain't,

Now I say I haven't seen you anywhere,

I'm hurting,

But I don't want to be bait.

- The silent suffering

- Broken -

I don't know what to say, but trust me my heart leaks, my heart breaks, piece by piece, part by part, cell by cell. I feel alone. I feel worthless. You walked through that door, and I told myself I wouldn't catch feelings. I told myself... that'd you'd be nothing more than just a friend, now you walk out that same door, taking my heart with you.

The farther you walk away from the door, the more my broken soul heals. I can scream for relief but sometimes it never comes. Despite what you say, despite what you did, I won't ever love you again.

One day I will get over you, no one has put me through as much pain as you have, but I won't let these memories distract me from the greater good. If you caused me pain then even the Lord knows you weren't the one for me. With patience comes time, and with time comes relief.

It don't matter to me what you tryna say,

I swear you said you loved me,

But now you tryna say you didn't like me that way,

You said we we're meant to be,

But now you don't even notice me during the night or day.

I'm all alone,

No one's dialled my phone,

That's when I realised,

I got this,

I have hope,

I'm as hard as a stone.

- *The overcomer*

- Everything Will Be Okay -

Whatever has happened has happened. They made you feel happy, but what's better? Temporary or permanent happiness? The way he/she looked at you, engraved in your mind isn't it? But do you remember the times you were happy? The times you were laughing uncontrollably? Do you? You forgot, we all do, we always focus on the negatives rather than the positives, but if you forgot the times you were happy, then you will surely forget his/her eyes. You may think he/she was the one, but if they really were the "one", why'd they leave? Never blame yourself for them leaving you, you are precious, needed and a warrior. People will blame you because they can't think of any other excuse to leave you. It's never actually you. I go back to my point, why'd they leave? Because they didn't deserve you, you are way too precious. If they couldn't see it, forget them! You deserve the best of the best, and he/she was not the best, I promise you that.

Today I rise,

I rise from the ashes,

I rise from the same building you burnt,

I rise from a pain equivalent to 1000 lashes,

I rise from the dirt,

I rise,

Higher... and higher.

- The ascension

- Getting You Out My Head -

Life goes on what can you do, I remember the times I loved you, I swear to myself I will be okay, you hurt me, and I loved you? I was such an idiot. The love you provided was nothing more than a deception. A sugar-coated lie. I try hard, harder than I ever have to forget you. But how can I? After you made me feel as if I was on top of the peak, as if I was the best person to live. I loved you so much. But the love you provided… was nothing more than a deception. A sugar-coated lie. For that you don't deserve a single drop of my love.

I'm broken,

But there isn't a single thing that can't be fixed.

Human kind has survived for centuries, so can I, this ain't the end of me, and I will always prevail.

I fall apart,

A tear right down my heart,

But I shouldn't have trusted you at the start,

You left, you done your part.

I ain't ever going back.

- A survivor of heartbreak

- Enough -

I've kept your name on the tip of my tongue for too long, I've been suffering in silence for too long, enough is enough. It's time I moved on, it's time I pursued my happiness, it's time I dig my feet into the ground and scream in happiness. It's do or die, my happiness is everything, nothing will come in my way, especially you tearing me apart, breaking me apart, ripping me apart. You hurt me, but you won't do it again, hurt me once you definitely won't hurt me twice. I'm not the type to make amends. You're in the past, what awaits… is my future, a bright future filled with happiness and smiles. Oh, and you're not invited.

"Do not dwell in the past as that has gone, but focus on what is to come as that is your future"

"Never regret yesterday. Life is in you today, and you make your tomorrow."

~ L. Ron Hubbard

CHAPTER 4

Loving Yourself

I was told I was ugly,

A monster,

Only find a partner if I was lucky,

They say happiness isn't on my roster,

… But they're wrong.

I got a soul of gold,

A personality that's bold,

I don't care what I'm told,

…

Because I'm on top of the world.

- Useless voices

- Self Confidence -

No one knows us as well as we know ourselves. Call me ugly, call me stupid, you don't know me. Truth is no one does. Truth is no one knows us, only we... know us. People can call us stupid, they can call us ugly, they can say whatever the hell they want, but do they know us? Hell no, then how the hell do they have the cheek to say anything about us! We are our own kingdom, our own palace, no one knows the doors, the paths, the hallways better than you do.

You are amazing, you are beautiful, you are benevolent, why am I reminding you? Nowadays life moves on so fast we forget who we are. We forget how amazing we are, we forget everything. People are moving fast, they forget we even exist. So it's important that you remember, you are on top of the damn world.

Enough going with the flow, time we left a legacy.

My heads a mess,

Probably because I'm at my best,

More love,

Hate less,

I'm above your hate,

You can't hurt me anymore,

Nah, it's too late.

Success is the only thing in my fate,

So if you see me doing something other than succeeding,

You're in the wrong dimension.

- Immunity

- Satisfaction -

Happiness isn't easy to find, but it's much easier to find if you're happy with yourself, self-confidence is one of the most important factors to finding happiness. Are you satisfied with yourself? Never succumb to the treacherous words of those who have a hateful tongue. Rather surround yourself with those who speak with a humble passion. Surround yourself with those who make you feel loved, special and unique.

You deserve nothing but happiness, laughter and success.

Only the people around you can make you feel satisfied about yourself. Being satisfied about yourself is more important than you can imagine. Be proud of your body, your skin, your looks, your personality, everything. No matter what anyone says, and if anyone says anything… ignore them. Sometimes silence is the most powerful weapon.

You hardly know me,

So why don't you leave me alone,

Instead of speaking bad about me,

Let me be,

Because there ain't nothing to see,

- Don't speak on my name.

- Fake Fear -

I fear to be an outcast. I fear society will abandon me because I'm useless.

But reality dictates society doesn't know me, but I know it [society].

Then why does this imaginary fear roam around my empty corridors. I feel like I'm useless because I haven't found myself yet. I still feel the emptiness at large, or do I? It takes time. Patience is vital. But I will find myself. Maybe I have but I've been blind to myself this whole time?

It's time I finish what I complete. I've been searching for happiness in all 4 corners of the world. I gave up but I will never lose faith, society cannot stop me from finding my happiness, so it's from this hour... that I get back on the hunt.

"Never let the whispers of society talk themselves into your brain"

I'm a warrior,

A survivor.

A human,

Learning from the mistakes,

I become stronger,

Forever.

But most importantly,

I am the king of the world,

Ain't nothing better than me,

Nor is anything lower than me.

- Addicted to the humble confidence.

"To fall in love with yourself is the first secret to happiness."

~ Robert Morely

"Love yourself unconditionally, just as you love those closest to you despite their faults."

~ Les Brown

CHAPTER 5

Changes

A new me,

The old me has vanished,

Depression and sadness were never meant to be,

Negativity has been banished,

Success is what is to come,

So make sure you watch and see... what I become.

- The beginning of a light

- The Beginning of a Masterpiece -

Today, is the day I shed my old self, my old self was filled with negativity, it can't remain. Today, I construct myself from the bottom up. Today... I show the world what I'm capable of.

Sometimes change is good, sometimes it's awful. But that's a risk I'm willing to take, would I rather rock these weathered boots or be in a nice pair of sneakers? In whatever stance, the new is better than the old.

No longer do I look at what I am today but I look at what I want to be tomorrow, what I want to be in 5,10,20 years from now. I don't want to be the same person who puts up a smile for people but comes home and drowns in sorrow. That's over.

A new day...

A new me...

A new beginning.

My sadness lays in a body bag,

My happiness reveals as the night turns into day,

I wake up every day with the things I got,

Each thing makes grateful for everything in every way,

Each day is a war, but each day I raise my flag,

Each day I rise higher than an astronaut.

- The positive flow

- Waiting -

I await the day I can say I'm happy, but for that, do I need to change myself? I'm so clueless, my mind is in the midst of a storm. I never know what to do. I lived my life waiting for the things I loved to come to me. I loved the moments I was smiling, jumping in laughter. Those memories are nothing but a blur. The little things are always the biggest things. A little smile could make my day, why… why do I remain so miserable? Change is never the easiest thing. But it's the best looking thing.

So I did. I changed. I left my miserable self behind. Spread the word that happiness is just a step away, I changed completely. Like a snake shedding its old skin only to be reborn into a renewed shell. A brighter, better skin. Sometimes it's what we humans have to do too, change completely, for the better.

Umar Ashraf

I just flipped the switch,

The light just entered the dark,

And I didn't even twitch,

Positivity is what I talk,

Humbly is how I walk,

I don't care if I'm poor or rich,

… I'm happy.

- Never stop.

- Resilient -

A change is a change, but now it's up to you to see whether this 'change' suits you or not, do you love your new self? Do you love how you are? Remember self-love is most important when changing. If people can't accept you for who you are they aren't worth your time, but as long as you are fine with your new self, who cares what others say! But if you think this new self doesn't suit you, don't change back… change into a newer better person, it's never too late to change yourself for the better. Be strong, never lose hope, and be resilient. Never ever change yourself based on what you see on social media, you'll see fashion models and other celebrities etc. and you may be blinded by their success. But two people can never go down the same path, we all have our own roads, so change yourself based on your requirements and your

"Yesterday I was clever, so I wanted to change the world. Today I am wise, so I am changing myself."

~ Rumi

CHAPTER 6

Peace

Umar Ashraf

The melody of nature's dwellers,

My heart comes to peace,

The wind whistles through the bristles of the trees,

My pain seems to decrease,

I finally feel home, at ease.

From the tides and storms,

To the lakes and streams,

From the snowstorms,

To the peaceful extremes,

My heartbeats… at ease.

- The cleared mist

- The Earth Sings -

The world keeps moving, but sometimes we don't move along with it. But the world isn't perfect. There's war, there's peace. Instead of dwelling on the wars, we need to address the wars within us. Peace is the medicine to war. There isn't a disease that can't be cured. Don't believe me?

"There is no disease that Allah has created, except that He also has created its treatment."

— Prophet Muhammad (Peace be upon him)

The world's forests, mountains, lakes, rivers, ravines, creeks, streams, all of this beauty we have been blessed with, is a cure to your internal wars. Sometimes it's best that we zone out and focus only on what is in front of us. And breathe.

Be at peace with yourself. Only then can you thrive.

The pure air,

The towered mountains,

The forest sings a peaceful prayer,

The natural surroundings,

An end to all despair.

- *The Wanderer.*

- Wandering -

I'm just a wanderer, in search of my peace. Water gushes through the cracks within the weathered rock. Wind rushes through the empty valleys, whilst I sit on a cliff breathing in the purest air known to mankind, my heart rests for once. All internal conflicts come to an eternal ceasefire. I raise my arms to the sky, thanking the lord for the blessings He has given us, to be fair, we only see what He has given us after we come out of our shell. The clouds dissipate into the clear sky, the sun wave's goodbye, my eyes tear a waterfall. My knees collapse due to the sheer beauty, a beauty so blinding, so precious, and so delicate…A treasure.

Peace.

Umar Ashraf

At ease, at rest,

Nature thrives from the eastern coasts to the west,

But as humanity grows,

We notice it less and less,

Out there, there is a burning rose…

Filled with despair and sorrow,

She doesn't realise the mercy around her,

From the sands of the Sahara to the snow on Mount Kilimanjaro,

Nature, the cure that cleanses a blur,

Oh, the peace nature provides.

- The fire fighter.

- The Extinguished Fire -

Nature truly helps with pain. Sometimes we forget to breathe and the pain consumes us internally, if we aren't mentally fit you will never fully be physically fit. That's why it's important we exterminate that uneasiness within your soul. At times that can be as simple as just sticking your head out the window and taking a deep breath, filling your lungs and extending your ribs. We don't realise it but a fresh breath of air can refresh your whole mind. Think of it as a computer, once you refresh the screen it works much better, doesn't it? That's the same way us humans work. You need to remember to breathe, and that can actually ease your discomfort. Nature is your best friend, but is it yours?

The melody sings its way into my heart,

The instruments are set off with one strike,

Peace prospers through my body,

The peaceful art,

I no longer feel as if I was broken apart,

Rather I was fixed, piece by piece, and part by part.

- The musical therapy

- The Venomous Melody -

You never would've thought that the music you were listening to had an impact on your mental health. But it does. Everything I write in this book I write from experience, one of my mistakes was that I would listen to depressing music and that would never help. It only made me feel more depressed and more saddened, almost knee deep in my own tears to be honest. Once I switched to soothing peaceful music I realised to utilize everything, my body moved with the flow of the music, it wasn't toxic, rather it was useful. I finally felt useful for once and my choice of music was at the centre of it. So if anything, if you want to be at peace, listen to soothing music not depressing music. Not only can it end your depression but it can also bring a lot of productivity into your life. Enough sitting around its time we did something, don't you think?

Tell me, was it worth it?

Being someone else?

Don't you like being free?

How did it feel living under a microscope?

A life where people based you on a "horoscope",

Being sat down, tied to a rope?

So tell me, was it worth it?

- Be yourself.

- The Bright Light -

My soul breathes, a calamity comes to seize. There's a fire chasing me, burning everything in its way, I kept tripping, it was growing with more rage. I was just a wanderer, in search of my peace. But peace is like finding a needle in a haystack. At times my soul surrendered, my knees planted within the deep soils. The fire was getting closer, I could feel it… closer than my own sweat. I kept running. Dashing through the bushes and trees of the evergreen forest. The sky felt as if it was crashing upon me, my breathing became even more rapid, my heartbeat was too fast, a total system failure was imminent. Or so I thought…

I guess we have to go through pain to realise what happiness is.

Suddenly, the fire stopped advancing. Clouds swirled and constructed themselves above the furious blaze. One rain drop after another and suddenly a storm of happiness attacked with no mercy. The fire… extinguished. As for the man… his story continues.

CHAPTER 7

Expectations

I was expected to do everything,

Wasn't allowed to do anything,

I can sleep but I can't rest,

I'm expected to be the best,

An anvil on my chest,

Always expected to pass every test,

But why am I treated different from the rest?

What did I do to deserve less?

- Captivity.

- Burden -

This weight on my shoulders causes my knees to cave in. My head filled with explosives on a timer set to explode. I scream "enough!" but my voice is silenced. Piece by piece my freedom is being taken from me. A zip put to shut my mouth, my legs and hands chained, the key thrown away. I was being expected too much of, by my own kin, by my friends, by anyone who decided to look my way. The world keeps rotating on its axis but my head rotates the other way. Oh my… it feels like someone's jumping on my chest, I sleep but deep within I find no peace, no rest. I can eat but I still feel hungry. I can give my all but I'm still expected to do more. It's like I've ran a kilometre but I'm told I only took one step. They want me to run the kilometre but why does it feel so long? Why does it not end?

… And when I'm tired, they seize everything. An embargo… A blockade. I'm a prisoner in my own world.

They slash my legs and tell me to run more…

Now tell me, are they not asking too much? Or was I born to be a slave to orders?

I am who I am,

I am not less,

Nor am I more,

I try to be the best,

But you work me too hard, got me fighting a war,

Despite what you do or what you say,

I am who I am,

No matter how grey you make my day,

I am who I am,

Even if you try to lead me astray from the righteous way,

I will be... who I am.

- Strong and steady.

- Acceptance -

Accept yourself, never anyone else's version of you. You are you, they are themselves. They can expect you to be everything, but you got to show them the line. Take it easy, never rush yourself to meet other people's expectations. Take your time. Set your goals and meet them, your goals are your own expectations of yourself. Set the bar to a level you know you can hit. But gradually keep raising the bar, that is the way of success. You don't owe anyone anything so don't let them boss you around. Never be anyone's slave. You were born free, you were born with the right to freedom, happiness and success. Never expect things from anyone as well, because they never deliver to your expectations. Be solo. Be free. Be a lone wolf... be you.

Without anyone else.

And remember...

You are amazing, you are a king/queen, and you are you. There ain't nothing better than you.

So don't be sad if you fall once. Because you'll rise 100x higher.

People expect too much,

And you forget your worth,

You forget your own sense of touch,

But in the end we all surrender to the same earth,

Were just different at birth,

But that doesn't mean were of less worth than the other,

At the end everyone is your sister or your brother,

Just from different mothers.

- A worth no currency can buy.

- Expecting from Others -

There's so many thoughts going through my brain. I trusted you with my life and you threw it away with your used clothes. Is that how little you think of me? Maybe it was me expecting anything from you in the first place.

Usually nowadays we expect so much from others, why? One of the ways in which we are socialized by our parents/guardians growing up is that they reward us or punish us for our behaviour. What happens is that we grow up looking towards others expecting an evaluation of our behaviour. If it was only our behaviour it would be okay but often we look towards others for an evaluation of ourselves as a whole. Am I a good person? Am I a bad person? Do I have the right to exist?

Many of us end up constantly looking into other people's eyes to find out who we are.

You know yourself better than anyone else, so never go asking other people about their opinion of you, they can never give you the right answer.

It's a marvellous day,

Freedom and air,

A gift I thought of as rare,

I ain't going back to the old days,

Suffocation and chains,

The thought of what life was makes me sick,

To be taken for granted,

Instead of happiness I tasted numerous pains,

But those days are gone,

A tree of happiness has been planted,

With that… my future has been drawn.

- The new beginning.

Umar Ashraf

- Survival -

Imagine a world, where we'd sacrifice ourselves for the betterment of the other. Imagine a world where we share what we earn, imagine a world where we spread happiness instead of hate. Imagine a world where we have peace instead of war, handshakes instead of conflict, and hugs instead of punches. Imagine a world like that. Imagine smiles on everyone's faces. Imagine such a positive world, my heart almost tears.

Instead we live in a harsh world, a harsh reality. A world with a lack of positivity, a world where you have to have your guard up all the time. A world where your own family, your own friends take you for granted. Surviving in this world is harder than we thought it was. It's always been difficult. But as the years count the difficulty rises. But we got to learn how to cope. How?

Don't trust the people who broke your trust. Don't get into company that causes an ill feeling within your gut. Don't rely on anyone because they'll just let you fall. Rise because you are strong, even if you say you aren't we both know deep down that you are. So rise like a true warrior and finish your conquest to find your happiness, and never let anyone or anything get in your way.

I was expected to fail

I proved them wrong the minute I was born,

They didn't see it then,

They didn't want to get to know me, just specific details,

I was the rose deep within the thorns,

But they thought they were the rose and I was the thorns,

But I'm still gonna prove them wrong all over again.

- Proving them wrong since '02

"I'm not in this world to live up to your expectations and you're not in this world to live up to mine."

~ Bruce Lee

CHAPTER 8

The Religion of Islam

It is He who sees what is seen and unseen,

It is He who hears what can be heard and what can't be heard,

It is He, the creator of deen,

It is He who can set you backwards or forward.

- He is Allah SWT.

- Ya Allah -

My eyes water thinking about your mercy, your love and your generosity. Oh Allah, the tide sweeps the ground at my feet away, Oh Allah, I find it hard to go on until tomorrow. Oh Allah save what's left of me because I'm tired and worn from the tides and storms.

Patience.

Allah has three answers to a dua, "yes", "yes but not now", and "I've got something better for you". Allah SWT never rejects your dua, it is always heard. Dua's are accepted the most when:

— The last third of the night

— During the prayer: The closest a believer is to his Lord is when he is in a state of prostration.

— During the month of Ramadan.

— Laylat-ul-Qadr, on the night of the decree.

— While visiting the sick.

Umar Ashraf

The Prophet Muhammad SAW reported that the devil said to Allah: "I shall continue to lead Thy servants astray as long as their spirits are in their bodies." And Allah replied: "(Then) I shall continue to pardon them as long as they ask My forgiveness."

Recorded in Tirmidthi, Hadith 742

- I Remember -

I remember the times I drowned in my own sorrow, I remember the times I thought I was alone. Then your hand came from above. You said if I walk toward you, you will run towards me. Oh Allah you were right. Please forgive me for the times I wandered astray, for the times it was your faith I would betray, Oh Allah guide me to the right path, the right way! You are the one with all power, the protector, the provider and the ever so merciful. So Ya Allah give me peace! And remove these demons from my soul! Indeed you are

لَا تَحْزَنْ إِنَّ اللّٰهَ مَعَنَا

"Do not be sad, indeed Allah is with us"

[9:40 – Quran]

- A Dua for Ridding Depression -

'Abdullāh ibn Mas'ūd (may Allah be pleased with him) reported that the Prophet ﷺ said, "No person suffers any anxiety or grief, and then says:

"O Allah, I am your slave, the son of your slave and the son of your maid-slave. Your command over me is forever executed and Your decree over me is just. I ask you by every Name belonging to You, which You have Named Yourself with, or revealed in Your Book, or You taught to any of Your creation, or You have preserved in the knowledge of the unseen with You, that You make the Qur'ān the life of my heart and the light of my chest, and a departure for my sorrow and a release for my anxiety) except that Allah will remove his sorrow and replace it with happiness."

They asked, "O Messenger of Allah, should we memorize these phrases (of the supplication)?" He responded, "Yes, whoever hears these words should memorize them."

Recorded by Ahmed (4167), al-Hākim (1809), and Ibn Hibbān (984)

مَا يُرِيدُ اللّهُ لِيَجْعَلَ عَلَيْكُمْ مِنْ حَرَجٍ وَلَكِنْ يُرِيدُ لِيُطَهِّرَكُمْ وَلِيُتِمَّ نِعْمَتَهُ عَلَيْكُمْ لَعَلَّكُمْ تَشْكُرُونَ

"Allah does not want difficulty for you, but He wants to purify you, and to complete His favor upon you, that you may be grateful."

[Quran – 5:6]

- Hadith -

A man asked permission of the Prophet SAW (to take part) in a jihad (a battle against oppressors). The Prophet SAW asked, "Are your parents living?" He said, "Yes." The Prophet SAW said, "Then go to them and do jihad (by taking care of them)."

Recorded in Bukhari, Muslim, Tirmidthi, Abu Daud

Always be kind to your parents, SubhanAllah.

لَا يُكَلِّفُ اللّهُ نَفْسًا إِلاَّ وُسْعَهَا رَبَّنَا لَا تُؤَاخِذْنَا إِنْ نَسِينَا أَوْ أَخْطَأْنَا رَبَّنَا وَلَا تَحْمِلْ عَلَيْنَا إِصْرًا كَمَا حَمَلْتَهُ عَلَى الَّذِينَ مِنْ قَبْلِنَا رَبَّنَا وَلَا تُحَمِّلْنَا مَا لَا طَاقَةَ لَنَا بِهِ وَاعْفُ عَنَّا وَاغْفِرْ لَنَا وَارْحَمْنَا أَنْتَ مَوْلَانَا فَانصُرْنَا عَلَى الْقَوْمِ الْكَافِرِينَ

"Allah does not burden a soul except [with that within] its capacity. "Our Lord, and burden us not with that which we have no ability to bear. And pardon us; and forgive us; and have mercy upon us. You are our protector, so give us victory over the disbelieving people."

[Quran – 2:286]

- Be Kind to One Another -

"None of you will have true faith till he wishes for his (Muslim) brother what he likes for himself."

Recorded by: Bukhari, Iman (Faith), 7; Muslim, Iman (Faith), 71

"A Muslim is a brother of another Muslim, so he should not oppress him, nor should he hand him over to an oppressor. Whoever has fulfilled the needs of his brother, Allah will fulfil his needs; whoever has brought his (Muslim) brother out of a discomfort, Allah will bring him out of the discomforts of the Day of Resurrection, and whoever has screened a Muslim, Allah will screen him (of his faults) on the Day of Resurrection."

Recorded by: Bukhari, Mazalim (Injustices), 3; Muslim, Birr (Piety), 58

CHAPTER 9

The End of a Journey

A new era has arrived,

The time of sadness has ticked past,

A time I have survived,

But for now, happiness, at last.

My face bears a smile,

Something that wasn't there a few months back,

But I swear I'm gonna wear this smile every other mile,

This is a new era, ain't no going back.

- A new era.

- Committed -

I'm done complaining, if I ain't where I want to be, I'm gonna knuckle down. I may get knocked down but I ain't gonna stay on the floor, I will rise up, get up, stronger each time. Never give up, on repeat in my mind. I may feel helpless but hell no, I will never give up. I will never start something and give up half way. I finish everything I started. I am committed to making the life I want, and I refuse to believe in so called limitations. I believe that I can do anything my mind wills.

With belief comes action, with belief comes possibilities, and with belief comes opportunities'. So hell no, I will follow my heart, I'm done reaching around me, I'm reaching for the stars. If you believe it, you can achieve it, if you can dream it, you can sure as hell be it. Achieving anything of significance in life is not easy, but the only way you can guarantee achieving nothing is not trying in the first place. It may not happen right away, but if you are committed and maintain the belief that you will attain your desired outcome. Then you will attain your desired outcome! Never give up, never ever give

Filled with all this positivity,

Dedicated to making changes,

Ending all negativity,

A smile ever so contagious,

Tick-tock, times running out,

Life's a bit too short,

So it's time I chose a different route.

- Taking responsibility.

- The Big Push -

I refuse to believe we are stuck. That we are out of luck, that we are worthless, useless, and pathetic. Now is the time we rise out of bed with a fresh mind-set each day. Rising above our personal limitations. Each day is my day, whether that be today, tomorrow, or the day after tomorrow, I live to rule, not to be ruled.

There is no depression, anxiety, or any other disorder that will roam within my soul. I came out of the storm stronger than I ever have been. But never again will I enter the same storm twice. Starting today, I will do everything and anything in my power to make each day a productive day. No more sobbing or weeping, its time I did something, even spreading smiles. I ain't gonna let a brother or a sister suffer in silence. No more suffering, for me, for you, for anyone. Enough is enough.

'I hated every minute of training, but I said, 'Don't quit. Suffer now and live the rest of your life as a champion.'

~ Muhammad Ali

- From Healing to Healed -

This journey has almost come to end. But the end to one thing, is always the beginning to something else. Evaluate yourself. How do you feel now? Has anything changed? If not make sure you change something. If your old self was upset then it can't remain. A new beginning, a new you.

Your commitment has to be dedicated to self-development, not self-destruction. How bad do you want it? How dedicated are you to achieving greatness? The world may be negative, but that doesn't mean you have to be. I am ugly, I am fat, I am worthless, NO, you are not. Change that "I am" to I am amazing, I am beautiful, I am great, those are the words that will fuel your life. I've fallen over and over again but I've rose to succeed. Focus on what you have not the things you want, focus on the people who love you not those that hate you. Shape your mind-set, and you'll shape your life. Do what you need now, stop doubting yourself, stop letting others bring you down. Life is hard, but if you do those hard things that no one else is willing to do, then life will be easy. Rewrite your own history, stop waiting for others to pick you up, make your life perfect, and make your life great, only you can do that. Don't depend on anyone else. Have faith in yourself.

Now and then it's good to pause in our pursuit of happiness and just be happy.

~ Guillaume Apollinaire

CHAPTER X

The Beginning of the Road to Success

Umar Ashraf

Happiness in my veins,

Now is the time to stride forward,

One step at a time is how you make gains,

Success is my motto from now onwards.

- The start of a future

- Success -

In life we can choose to sit around or we can do something, we can give up or we can succeed, we can be average or we can be at the top of the class. I think we've had enough of sitting around. It's not your fault either, mental disorders such as depression or anxiety can limit our success due to its impact on the person. But we can definitely overcome those limitations. We can overcome anything we put our mind to, people survived in caves for god's sake, if they could do it, then why the hell can't we? Us humans, we work best when our survival is at stake. Under a roof, getting food, getting clothes, our survival doesn't seem to be compromised? But now what if I took that house away, what if you only had one pair of clothes, what if you only had one meal every two days. It's only at that moment when you start working hard to get every little penny. What if you put that effort in before?

You can stop this. Put the effort in now and you won't have to suffer later on.

Today I may not have anything,

Tomorrow I may not have much,

But one day I will have something,

Never giving up is everything.

Succeeding is my new way of life,

It doesn't always have to be about money,

A confidence sharper than a knife,

Success can be like going from a citizen to the head of a country,

Success is the way we go forwards,

Striving onwards.

- Improving.

- Real Success -

Success; the accomplishment of an aim or purpose. In order to succeed you must set your goals, your aims. Every day when you wake up, plan what you're going to do. Each time you do something you planned, tick it off your list. It's almost as if a burden is being relieved off your shoulders. You can never succeed going in blind. Success is a victory. You can plan for a victory, you can prepare for it. But if you go in blind, will you come out victorious?

"There are no secrets to success. It is the result of preparation, hard work, and learning from failure."

- Colin Powell

"Success seems to be connected with action. Successful people keep moving. They make mistakes, but they don't quit."

- Conrad Hilton

"If you really want to do something, you'll find a way. If you don't, you'll find an excuse."

- Jim Rohn

- The End of the Road -

All journey's come to end. From each journey we learn something, more importantly we realise who we are, we realise the tiny details that make us, us. Question yourself after every journey. What have I accomplished? How could I have made it better? How did this journey help me?

Through life we have numerous journeys. Each with a purpose. We get tired. We give up, but no, no more. Enough. No more stopping halfway, always complete what you start.

I hope you can finally say that "I am happy", I hope that you can smile without forcing it and most importantly I hope whatever depression, anxiety and any other mental disorder within your soul has been expelled.

Don't live your life in fear, you won't be able to enjoy it.

"The most important thing is to enjoy your life, to be happy, it's all that matters."

— Audrey Hepburn

THE END

This journey may have come to an end,
but more journeys await you.

34183831R00059

Printed in Great Britain
by Amazon